Having a
Mary Heart
in a Martha
World

STUDY GUIDE

Having a Mary Heart in a Martha World

Finding Intimacy *with* God
in the
Busyness *of* Life

JOANNA WEAVER

WATERBROOK
PRESS

HAVING A MARY HEART IN A MARTHA WORLD STUDY GUIDE
PUBLISHED BY WATERBROOK PRESS
12265 Oracle Boulevard, Suite 200
Colorado Springs, Colorado 80921

Trade Paperback ISBN 978-0-307-73160-9
eBook ISBN 978-0-307-73165-4

Cover design by Mark D. Ford

Published in the United States by WaterBrook Multnomah, an imprint of the Crown Publishing Group,
a division of Penguin Random House LLC, New York.

WATERBROOK and its deer colophon are registered trademarks of Penguin Random House LLC.

Printed in the United States of America
2016

10 9 8 7

SPECIAL SALES
Most WaterBrook Multnomah books are available at special quantity discounts when purchased in bulk by
corporations, organizations, and special-interest groups. Custom imprinting or excerpting can also be done
to fit special needs. For information, please e-mail SpecialMarkets@WaterBrookMultnomah.com or call
1-800-603-7051.

Contents

Letter from Joanna

*W*ith so many wonderful Bible studies available, I'm honored that you have chosen my book *Having a Mary Heart in a Martha World: Finding Intimacy with God in the Busyness of Life.*

When my publisher suggested I expand the original Bible study and add video sessions, I was excited! After spending so long thinking about and studying the lives of Mary and Martha, two sisters Jesus considered dear friends, I'm delighted to share with you what I've learned. From their encounter with the Savior, I believe we can discover rich insights and deep truths that have the power to change our lives.

For God longs for relationship with you, my friend. It is the purpose for which you and I were made. And it is the purpose for which Jesus came to earth—so that, through His death and resurrection, we might be reconciled to a Father who loves us more than we could ever imagine. A Father who has provided everything necessary so that you and I could daily experience His presence. Right here and right now. Smack dab in the busyness of life.

I'm excited to take this journey with you. Something beautiful happens when we take time to sit at Jesus' feet, individually and corporately. As we make ourselves available, He makes Himself known to us. As we pour out our hearts in sweet communion, Jesus pours His life into us.

So take off your apron and lay aside your duties for a while. Come enjoy the incredible invitation of friendship Jesus extended to Mary and Martha—and to you and me as well.

Come discover the secret to having a Mary heart in a Martha world.

Becoming His,

Joanna Weaver

"I will give them a heart to know me, that I am the LORD. They will be my people, and I will be their God."

JEREMIAH 24:7

How to Use This Study

Having a Mary Heart in a Martha World—The Book

While you'll learn a great deal from watching the video sessions and completing the study guide homework, please be sure to read your assigned chapters in *Having a Mary Heart in a Martha World* prior to each week's discussion. The book provides the framework of this study and is necessary to your getting the most out of our time together.

As early in the study week as possible, you'll want to complete your assigned reading with a pen or highlighter in hand. I encourage you to mark or underline things that really speak to you—verses, quotes, stories, or analogies. Make notes in the book margins of any thoughts, questions, or revelations you'd like to discuss or share in class.

The Study Guide

After you've read the assigned portion in the book, begin to work through the questions and exercises in this guide. They are designed to help you reflect on God's Word and apply it. (Please note that I quote primarily from the 1984 edition of the New International Version, and most questions are shaped around that translation.)

Each week's lesson also includes:

- a *"Word Time" sidebar*. These are designed to give you tools to go deeper in your Bible study. Corresponding videos will be shown in class if there is time. (Videos can also be accessed at www.having amaryheart.com.)

- a *"Make a Plan" assignment*. Each week, you'll be encouraged to come up with action steps to apply the truths you've learned as you follow through on that plan during the upcoming week.

- *a memory verse.* Over the course of the study, you'll be asked to memorize nine verses. If that seems too overwhelming, choose two or three verses to focus on. Don't worry; I'll share some memorizing techniques that have helped me!
- *a video guide.* With fill-in-the-blank prompts, these pages help capture key points from the DVD session so that you can refer to them later.
- *a "Closing Time" reflection.* At the end of each lesson you'll have a chance to respond to what the Lord has impressed on your heart throughout the week and in the teaching session.

Note to Leaders

On the third DVD, you'll find a comprehensive Leader's Guide designed to help you navigate the special features of this study as well as get the most out of your weekly time together. Just print the pages, and place them in a three-ring binder for easy use. The Leader's Guide includes:

- practical advice for leading Bible studies
- a list of DVD content, including bonus features and how to use them
- session-by-session scripts to help you lead the discussion for a two-hour class (with modifications for a one-hour class); includes video prompts and other activities
- optional eleven- or twelve-week study format using Bonus Session video and other material
- optional Retreat Guide providing the tools you'll need to create a special event, including promotional materials, suggested activities, and lots more

The Leader's Guide can also be downloaded at www.havingamaryheart. com, where other study helps are available, including memory verses, promotional videos, publicity pieces, and website graphics. You can explore my other books and upcoming video curriculums as well.

If you have any questions, please send me an e-mail by clicking on the "contact Joanna" link at www.havingamaryheart.com. I hope you'll send me an e-mail to let me know when your group will be doing the study. I'd treasure the opportunity to pray for you and inform you when any new products or study resources become available. I'd also love to hear about any creative ideas you're using as well as what God is doing in your group.

Introduction

As Jesus and his disciples were on their way, he came to a village where a woman named Martha opened her home to him. She had a sister called Mary, who sat at the Lord's feet listening to what he said.

LUKE 10:38–39

Having a Mary heart in a Martha world?

Is it really possible? More than ever, I am convinced it is. Jesus wants to meet with you as surely as He met with Mary and Martha that long-ago day in Bethany. He wants to reveal Himself to you, filling you with His presence and His love so that His grace spills through you to a dry and thirsty world.

Though our initial introduction to Mary and Martha is only four verses long, I believe this brief story has the power to literally change our lives. So let's begin!

As Jesus and his disciples were on their way, he came to a village where a woman named Martha opened her home to him. She had a sister called Mary, who sat at the Lord's feet listening to what he said. But Martha was distracted by all the preparations that had to be made. She came to him and asked, "Lord, don't you care that my sister has left me to do the work by myself? Tell her to help me!"

"Martha, Martha," the Lord answered, "you are worried and upset about many things, but only one thing is needed. Mary has chosen what is better, and it will not be taken away from her." (Luke 10:38–42)

Theme Verse

Come to me, all you who are weary and burdened, and I will give you rest.

MATTHEW 11:28

Discussion Questions

1. Before we begin this study, what preconceived ideas do you have about Mary and Martha? Which woman do you relate to most—Mary or Martha? Explain your answer.

2. One woman told me, "My life is like a blender—and it's stuck on frappe!" What inanimate object best describes how your life currently feels, and why?

3. Read Matthew 11:28. What do Jesus' words mean to you?

Having a Mary Heart in a Martha World

Behold, I stand at the door and knock. If anyone hears My voice and opens the door, I will come in to him and dine with him, and he with Me.

REVELATION 3:20, NKJV

The Story of Mary and Martha—the Story of You and Me, Luke 10:38–42

The Living Room Intimacy _____ God that we long for will never be found in Kitchen Service _____ God.

Discovering the Better Part

1. Martha opened her home (Luke 10:38).
   - preparations—*diakonia*—_____

2. Mary opened her heart (Luke 10:39).
   - She made _____ for time with Jesus.

   - She did the _____.

   - She _____ to Jesus.

The same invitation Jesus made to Martha is the invitation He makes to us:

"Come spend time with Me.... Allow My _____ to fill your life so that I can spill you to the world!"

I sense the Lord saying...

Make a Plan

God desires to transform you by the power of His Word. He wants to speak specific things to your heart over the next several weeks. What one thing could you do to get the most out of this study?

- Follow through with your week 1 "Make a Plan" homework.
- Read chapters 1 and 2 in *Having a Mary Heart in a Martha World*.
- Answer week 2 study questions.
- Memorize **Matthew 11:28**: "Come to me, all you who are weary and burdened, and I will give you rest."

A Tale of Two Sisters

But Martha was distracted by all the preparations that had to be made.
She came to him and asked, "Lord, don't you care that my sister has left
me to do the work by myself? Tell her to help me!"

LUKE 10:40

READ: Chapters 1 and 2 in *Having a Mary Heart in a Martha World*

ave you ever felt overworked and underappreciated?

I know I have. Feeling as if the weight of the world is on your shoulders is difficult, especially when no one seems inclined to share the load. The frustration Martha felt that day in Luke 10:38–42 is definitely not a foreign emotion to me! In fact, I've earned frequent-flyer elite-plus status when it comes to the emotional miles I've wasted on self-pity.

Aren't you glad we have a Savior who knows our human weaknesses yet loves us anyway? When Martha came barging into the living room and poured out her complaint to Jesus, she was on the right track. "Trust in him at all times, O people," the psalmist tells us in Psalm 62:8, "pour out your hearts to him, for God is our refuge." There is no better place to go than to Jesus with our troubles, our frustrations, and our perceived injustices.

But be sure to stick around for the answer. While Jesus may not give you what you want, He will always give you what you need. And that, my friend, is far more important than extra help in the kitchen!

Memory Verse

Come to me, all you who are weary and burdened, and I will give you rest.

MATTHEW 11:28

WORD TIME: Memorizing Scripture

Throughout this study, I've suggested a scripture to memorize and meditate on each week. Don't be intimidated; you can do this! Here's a method, adapted from the Navigators' 2:7 Discipleship Course,[1] that has really helped me hide God's Word in my heart.

- Write the verse (or verses) you want to memorize on an index card.
- Read the verse out loud several times.
- Learn the reference and first phrase of the verse together as a unit.
- Repeat the unit three times, then add the next phrase. Repeat that three times.
- Gradually add phrases and repeat the reference once again at the end.
- Always review the verse using the following pattern:

  REFERENCE—VERSE—REFERENCE
  For instance:
  "John 11:35, 'Jesus wept,' John 11:35."

- Don't forget to repeat the reference at the end—it's important!
- Focus on saying the verse word perfect.
- Review, review, review.

Scripture memorization doesn't come easily for most of us, but I can assure you, it will come if you persevere and practice! Don't give up. As you exercise your mind, your capacity for memorization will grow.

Why not start today? You'll find all of our study's memory verses on pages 107–8 for easy reference.

I have hidden your word in my heart that I might not sin against you.

PSALM 119:11

THIS WEEK'S STUDY

1. Read Luke 10:38–42. List at least two things you learn about Martha in this passage and at least two things you learn about Mary. How would you describe Martha in one word? How would you describe Mary?

MARTHA

1.

2.

One word: _____

MARY

1.

2.

One word: _____

2. The story of Mary and Martha stirs up memories of sibling rivalry for many of us. What battles with your siblings do you remember the most? What did you do to get your parents to notice you?

3. A woman told me, "I guess I'm just a Martha and that I'll always be a Martha." Is it possible for our basic character to change, or are we destined to remain stuck in a predetermined nature? Explain your answer.

4. All of us feel alone at times, even great heroes of the faith. Read 1 Kings
   19:1–18. How did the "Deadly D's" of distraction, discouragement, and
   doubt attack Elijah after the great victory over the prophets of Baal in
   1 Kings 18? I've completed the first one as an example:

   DISTRACTION: *Jezebel's anger made him run for his life.*

   DISCOURAGEMENT:

   DOUBT:

5. In this passage (1 Kings 19:1–18), how did God minister to Elijah in the
   midst of his discouragement? How has God ministered to you when you felt
   alone and were hurting?

6. In Mark 4:35–41 the disciples echoed Martha's question: "Don't you care?"
   What was the situation, and what can we learn from Jesus' response?

7. With Jesus' response in Mark 4 in mind, read Isaiah 43:1–2. What does this portion of Scripture teach us about the difficult times in our lives?

8. On page 22 (hardcover, page 27) of *Having a Mary Heart in a Martha World,* I wrote, "If [Satan] can't make us doubt God's existence, Satan will do his best to make us doubt God's love." Have the circumstances of your life ever made you question God's love for you? How did that affect your relationship with Him?

9. Use the following scale to describe how you currently feel about your walk with God. Don't be afraid to be honest.

RELIGION		**RELATIONSHIP**
Going through		**A growing**
motions		**friendship with God**

       1   2   3   4   5   6   7   8   9   10

10. Like Martha, we can open our homes in ministry and service yet allow our hearts to remain unengaged in what we are doing. The prophet Isaiah speaks of something similar in Isaiah 29:13. Write out that verse here.

11. Has any part of your relationship with God become routine? Are you doing things without engaging your heart? If so, write out a prayer here asking God to renew your passion for Him and His Word.

12. Read Psalm 103 through completely, considering the many ways God shows His love for us. Now go back and pick five that resonate in your life right now. (If you are struggling to know the Father's love, consider reading this psalm regularly so you won't forget "all his benefits.")

   •

   •

   •

   •

   •

   Which aspect of God's love means the most to you from this portion of scripture, and why?

Make a Plan

Mary's heart was fully opened to Jesus. She made room for Him in her life. What are some ways you could purposefully make time as well as room for God in your life this week? List your ideas here:

Now, choose the top three ideas, and number them in order of potential effectiveness.

1.

2.

3.

You have just discovered your action steps for the week! While you may not be able to implement them all, ask the Lord to help you make room in your heart as well as your life for time with Him.

Lord, Don't You Care?

Quick! Bring the best robe.... Let's have a feast and celebrate. For this son of mine was dead and is alive again; he was lost and is found.

LUKE 15:22–24

Another Set of Siblings, Luke 15:11–32

The Youngest Son

- "Father, give me my share" (verse 12).
- "He came to his _____" (verse 17).

The Father (verses 20–23)

- The father _____ him.
- The father _____ to him.
- The father restored him.

    "Best robe" conveys _____.

    Signet "ring" suggests _____.

    "Sandals" indicate _____.

    "Feast" signifies _____.

The Oldest Son

- "was in the field" (verse 25).
- "All these years I've been _____ for you" (verse 29).

Key Truths

1. Proximity doesn't ensure relationship.
2. God's love for others in no way diminishes His love for us.
3. We all need to come to our senses; it's time to come _____!

Our Father's heart: "Everything I have is _____" (Luke 15:31).

Notes

Closing Time

I sense the Lord saying…

Prayer Requests

This Week's Assignment

- Follow through with your week 2 "Make a Plan" homework.
- Read chapter 3 in *Having a Mary Heart in a Martha World*.
- Answer week 3 study questions.
- Continue to review Matthew 11:28. Memorize **Philippians 4:6–7**:
  "Do not be anxious about anything, but in everything, by prayer and petition, with thanksgiving, present your requests to God. And the peace of God, which transcends all understanding, will guard your hearts and your minds in Christ Jesus."

Week Three

❧

The Diagnosis

"Martha, Martha," the Lord answered, "you are worried and upset about many things."

LUKE 10:41

READ: Chapter 3 in *Having a Mary Heart in a Martha World*

Though we may not realize it, we are all affected by fear and worry. Whether it is the garden-variety kind of anxiety that crops up when the demands of life exceed our resources or a debilitating terror that haunts our nights and days, fear finds its way into our hearts and minds even as we try to push it away. But dear friend, we weren't wired for worry. We weren't fashioned for fear.

Over and over in the Bible, God tells us, "Do not be afraid; for I am with you" (for example, Genesis 26:24; Isaiah 43:5). I need that reminder. For when I focus on my circumstance rather than on God's assurance, I tend to worry, believing I am all alone. Perhaps that's why, more than 350 times in the Bible, God tells us in one manner or another to "fear not." Because giving way to fear slowly obliterates the sense of God's presence and systematically dismantles our faith in His love.

As you do this lesson, allow the Holy Spirit to shine the spotlight of heaven on any hidden pockets of fear in your life. Then give God permission to invade that space with His peace as you surrender your fears and set your mind on Him.

Memory Verse

Do not be anxious about anything, but in everything, by prayer and petition, with thanksgiving, present your requests to God. And the peace of God, which transcends all understanding, will guard your hearts and your minds in Christ Jesus.

PHILIPPIANS 4:6–7

WORD TIME: Bible Study Methods

Many of us want to go deeper in our study of God's Word, but we're unsure of *how* to study the Bible. I'd like to share a few methods I've found to be effective in my walk with God.

Topical Study—searches through Scripture to gain deeper insights into a specific subject

- Think of every form and synonym of the word or topic you want to study.

- Look up each word in a concordance or topical index.

- Read over the list of Scripture phrases that contain that word to find the verses that seem most relevant to your struggle, then look them up.

- Write out the verses that really speak to you. Consider memorizing one or two.

Book Study—focuses on one book of the Bible for an extended time

- Study the book's background, historical context, audience, and author.

- Read through the book quickly as an overview, then again slowly verse by verse.

- Look for common themes and/or repeated words.

- Explore cross references. Read various translations and commentaries.

Character Study—targets one specific person in the Bible (for example, David or Esther)

- Read portions of Scripture that directly involve the character and his or her story.

- List qualities, both good and bad; note growth or regression.

- Search for other biblical references to that person.

- Write down lessons learned and specific ways you are inspired.

Ask Questions—explores the passage of Scripture using the following queries:

- WHO wrote it and to whom was it written?

- WHAT is the overall theme?

- WHY was it written?

- WHERE did it take place?

- WHEN was it written?

> *Now the Bereans were of more noble character than the Thessalonians, for they received the message with great eagerness and examined the Scriptures every day to see if what Paul said was true.*
>
> ACTS 17:11

This Week's Study

1. Read Luke 10:40–41. Martha wanted Jesus to tell Mary to help out in the kitchen, but instead of giving her what she wanted, Dr. Jesus made a diagnosis: "Martha, Martha,...you are worried and upset about many things" (verse 41). If you had been Martha, how would Jesus' words have made you feel?

2. What types of things tend to worry and upset you?

3. According to Dr. Hallowell (see sidebar on the next page), more than half of us are chronic worriers. Which of the "Ten Signs of a Big Worrier" do you struggle with?

Ten Signs of a Big Worrier

Dr. Edward Hallowell, author of *Worry: Controlling It and Using It Wisely*, provides a checklist to help you determine if worry is a problem in your life.[2] Put a check mark in front of each description that is true of you to assess if you have a problem with worry.

____ You spend much more time in useless, nonconstructive worry than other people you know.

____ Other people comment on how much of a worrier you are.

____ You feel it is bad luck or tempting fate not to worry.

____ Worry interferes with your work: you miss opportunities, fail to make decisions, perform at a less-than-optimal level.

____ Worry interferes with your close relationships: your spouse and/or friends sometimes complain that your worrying is a drain on their energy and patience.

____ You know that many of your worries are unrealistic or exaggerated, yet you cannot seem to control them.

____ Sometimes you feel overwhelmed by worry and even experience physical symptoms such as rapid heart rate, rapid breathing, shortness of breath, sweating, dizziness, or trembling.

____ You feel a chronic need for reassurance even when everything is fine.

____ You feel an exaggerated fear of certain situations that other people seem to handle with little difficulty.

____ Your parents or grandparents were known as great worriers, or they suffered from an anxiety disorder.

Don't worry if you've checked a few more than you expected to. No matter to what degree worry is part of your nature, Jesus wants to set you free! He can change your heart and rewire your soul as you choose to trust God rather than give way to fear.

Search me, O God, and know my heart;
test me and know my anxious thoughts.

PSALM 139:23

4. Even if you are not a "big worrier," fear may affect you in less direct ways. Describe how fear might be related to the following areas:

Need to control:

Depression:

Regret from past:

Need for approval/success:

Anger:

Other:

5. Look up each of the following Bible verses, then draw a line from the Scripture reference and related Bible character to the statement that best describes each example of giving way to fear. (There may be more than one.)

Abraham, Genesis 12:12–13	Fear of people's opinions
Moses, Exodus 4:10, 13	Fear of failure
Twelve spies, Numbers 13:31–33	Fear of endangerment
Gideon, Judges 6:27	Fear of inadequacy
Servant who hid his talent, Matthew 25:24–25	Fear of circumstances

Describe a time when fear caused you to react in a way similar to one of the examples above.

6. Joshua 1:9 tells us how to live with courageous faith. Write out the verse in your own words.

7. Look at the chart below, which describes the differences between concern and worry:

CONCERN	WORRY
Involves a legitimate threat	Is often unfounded
Is specific (one thing)	Is generalized (spreads to many things)
Addresses the problem	Obsesses about the problem
Solves problems	Creates more problems
Looks to God for answer	Looks to self or others for answers

Consider a recent event or circumstance that has posed a personal challenge to you. Which column best characterizes your response?

How could knowing the difference between concern and worry change the way you approach problems in the future?

8. What do the following passages tell us to do with our worries and concerns, and what will be the result?

Proverbs 3:5–6
COMMAND:

ACTION(S):

RESULT:

Philippians 4:6–7
COMMAND:

ACTION(S):

RESULT:

9. Rewrite Matthew 6:25–30 as if God were speaking directly to you and the circumstance you identified in question 7 or another situation.

Therefore, I tell you, _____ [insert your name],

do not worry about _____

_____ [name your situation].… Look at the birds

of the air…the lilies of the field… _____

_____

_____

_____ [list ways God has been faithful to you].

10. Now read Matthew 6:31–34. Respond to this passage in a prayer to the Lord.

Lord, I don't want to worry as the world does. Help me…

Amen.

11. Look up Romans 8:35–36, and then list the various things that attempt to separate us from God's love but, according to Paul, cannot. Does the situation you noted in question 7 fit into one of these categories? (Example: A lost job might equate to "hardship.")

Now read Romans 8:37–39 aloud over your life and your situation. As an exercise of faith, jot down a brief summary of your problem, and then write the words "Conquered through Christ" across the description.

Freedom from Fear

> *For God has not given us a spirit of fear, but of power and of love and of a sound mind.*
>
> 2 TIMOTHY 1:7, NKJV

It All Started in the Garden, Genesis 2:7–3:24

Two Trees:

- The Tree of the Knowledge of Good and Evil
- The Tree of _____

The forbidden tree was a symbol of God's right to set _____ on our lives.

Progression of Temptation, Genesis 3:1–5

1. Doubt God's intentions (verse 1)
2. Doubt God's trustworthiness (verse 4)
3. Doubt God's motives (verse 5)

Adam and Eve stepped out from under God's _____—and fear entered the world.

Mistake #1: Eve engaged in a prolonged conversation with a talking snake.[3]

Mistake #2: Eve believed she _____ better than God.

The Remedy, Genesis 3:13–24

- God in His mercy _____ them (verse 21).
- God in His mercy barred them from the Tree of Life (verse 24).
- In His mercy, Jesus hung on a _____ to give us eternal life (Galatians 3:13).

Which tree will you eat from?

Make a Plan

When troubles arise, we tend to react rather than respond. Fear often drives those reactions. Think of a past circumstance to which you reacted in fear. How could you have better inserted God into the equation? In the future, what could you do differently to focus on faith rather than fear?

Using what you've discovered, make a plan for how you want to handle any adverse situations that might crop up this week:

Notes

Closing Time

I sense the Lord saying...

Prayer Requests

This Week's Assignment

- Follow through with your week 3 "Make a Plan" homework.
- Read chapter 4 in *Having a Mary Heart in a Martha World*.
- Answer week 4 study questions.
- Continue to review previous verses. Memorize **James 1:5**: "If any of you lacks wisdom, he should ask God, who gives generously to all without finding fault, and it will be given to him."

The Cure

Only one thing is needed. Mary has chosen what is better, and it will not be taken away from her.

LUKE 10:42

READ: Chapter 4 in *Having a Mary Heart in a Martha World*

*W*hen Jesus said, "Only one thing is needed…"

…it must have felt more like a curse than a cure. Just one more forgotten duty to add to Martha's never-ending to-do list. But Jesus' words were not an indictment of her service. His rebuke was an invitation to relationship. An offer to exchange the busyness and exhausting treadmill of good works for the one thing Martha's soul longed for. The only thing that could fill the emptiness of her heart—the "Better Part." The sweet gift of Jesus Himself.

The same invitation is made to you and me today. Because our good works, though important and needed, will never fill the void in our hearts created by the Fall. Only Jesus can restore all that we've lost. But we'll never discover what we've been missing until we slow down long enough to enjoy all that He wants to be to us.

So ignore the dust on the coffee table and set aside that to-do list. The Savior is calling your name.

Memory Verse

If any of you lacks wisdom, he should ask God,
who gives generously to all without finding fault,
and it will be given to him.

JAMES 1:5

WORD TIME: Reading and Marking Your Bible

If you don't yet have a Bible that you really enjoy and understand, I suggest that you look at the variety of translations available and consider upgrading to a study edition.

Then begin to make this Bible your own. Once I began to underline and highlight Scripture, my Bible became alive to me.

Here are some tips to enhance your reading and study experience:[4]

1. Ask the Holy Spirit to speak something fresh to your heart (Ephesians 1:17).

2. Read slowly, thinking of ways to apply to your life what you're reading.

3. Using a pen, colored pencil, or nonbleed highlighter, mark things that stand out to you, such as words of encouragement, insights, challenges, observations, etc.

4. While there are different methods, here are a few simple markings you can use:

   [Brackets]—put around a phrase or place them in the margin to note a specific portion.

   /Diagonal Lead-in and out/—use within the text or in the margin to mark a longer passage.

   Circle—use to emphasize repeated words in a passage or to indicate the principal characters or themes of that passage.

   Underline—use to highlight words, phrases, or a sentence.

When a verse really speaks to a situation I'm going through, I mark it with a star or a note in the margin to remind me of what God has said. This personal interaction with the Word of God has caused me to fall in love with the Bible even more.

I pray this exercise makes it come alive to you as well!

But his delight is in the law of the LORD,
and on his law he meditates day and night.

PSALM 1:2

Word Time Exercise

NOTE: This exercise will be done in class, after viewing the Word Time video "Reading and Marking Your Bible."

Using the tips offered on the previous page, read the following passage slowly and prayerfully, marking what speaks most to you.

ROMANS 12

Therefore, I urge you, brothers, in view of God's mercy, to offer your bodies as living sacrifices, holy and pleasing to God—this is your spiritual act of worship. [2] Do not conform any longer to the pattern of this world, but be transformed by the renewing of your mind. Then you will be able to test and approve what God's will is—his good, pleasing and perfect will.

[3] For by the grace given me I say to every one of you: Do not think of yourself more highly than you ought, but rather think of yourself with sober judgment, in accordance with the measure of faith God has given you. [4] Just as each of us has one body with many members, and these members do not all have the same function, [5] so in Christ we who are many form one body, and each member belongs to all the others. [6] We have different gifts, according to the grace given us. If a man's gift is prophesying, let him use it in proportion to his faith. [7] If it is serving, let him serve; if it is teaching, let him teach; [8] if it is encouraging, let him encourage; if it is contributing to the needs of others, let him give generously; if it is leadership, let him govern diligently; if it is showing mercy, let him do it cheerfully.

[9] Love must be sincere. Hate what is evil; cling to what is good. [10] Be devoted to one another in brotherly love. Honor one another above yourselves. [11] Never be lacking in zeal, but keep your spiritual fervor, serving the Lord. [12] Be joyful in hope, patient in affliction, faithful in prayer. [13] Share with God's people who are in need. Practice hospitality.

[14] Bless those who persecute you; bless and do not curse. [15] Rejoice with those who rejoice; mourn with those who mourn. [16] Live in harmony with one another. Do not be proud, but be willing to associate with people of low position. Do not be conceited.

[17] Do not repay anyone evil for evil. Be careful to do what is right in the eyes of everybody. [18] If it is possible, as far as it depends on you, live at peace with everyone. [19] Do not take revenge, my friends, but leave room for God's wrath, for it is written: "It is mine to avenge; I will repay," says the Lord. [20] On the contrary:

"If your enemy is hungry, feed him;
    if he is thirsty, give him something to drink.
In doing this, you will heap burning coals on his head."

[21] Do not be overcome by evil, but overcome evil with good.

This Week's Study

1. Do you ever feel your driven, perfectionistic, inner Martha Stewart coming out? List the ways she reveals herself.

2. Read the story of the wagon and the rocks on pages 48–51 of *Having a Mary Heart in a Martha World* (hardcover, pages 56–59). Take a look in your wagon. Draw and label the "rocks" that you are currently carrying.

3. Which of these rocks has God asked you to carry?

   Which rocks have you unwisely and sometimes unconsciously volunteered to carry for someone else?

4. Often the thing that weighs us down most is the feeling that we must bear the weight alone, that it is all up to us. What do we learn from each of the following verses?

   Psalm 46:1

   Psalm 68:19

   Isaiah 41:10

   1 Peter 5:7

5. As you read Luke 10:38–42, imagine being at Martha's home in Bethany. What do you think Jesus meant when He said that "only one thing" was needed?

6. Turn a few pages in your Bible to Luke 18:18–25, and read another conversation with Jesus.

What qualifications did the rich young ruler give for entering the kingdom of God?

What was the "one thing" Jesus said the young man lacked?

Why do you think Christ focused on his wealth?

Jesus' approach to people always seemed to vary. Why might the "one thing" God asks of you be different from what He requires of someone else?

7. Perhaps, like the rich young ruler, you've placed your hope in good works, in carrying more "rocks" as a way to earn more of God's love and favor. What do the following verses say about how we are saved, rescued from sin, and made acceptable in God's sight?

Romans 5:8–9

Titus 3:5

8. Read the story on page 56 of *Having a Mary Heart in a Martha World* (hardcover, page 64) about the birthday gift my husband gave me. I write: "So often we give God the gift we think He needs rather than take the time to find out what He desires." Why do you think we do this?

9. List the things that Titus 2:11–12 tells us the grace of God does in our lives:

Read on through verses 13–14. Who is the blessed hope, and what does He do for us?

How do these four verses encourage you?

10. Look up Isaiah 42:16. Write out the key things that God wants to do for you. Which one of these things means the most to you today, and why?

The Practical Power of the "One Thing"

The "one thing" that Jesus said was needed in Martha's life was fellowship with Him—and that's true for us too. But the principle of "one thing" also has smaller, practical implications that can help us when life feels overwhelming. Here are some ways to practice one-thing thinking when your wagon feels overloaded.

- *Invite Jesus to rule and reign.* Each morning before you get out of bed, invite the Lord to come take the throne of your life, to be your "one thing." Present your day to Him, and ask Him for wisdom and guidance.

- *Ask God to reveal the next step.* As you go through your day, keep asking the Lord, "What is the one thing I need to do next?" Don't let the big picture overwhelm you. Just take the next step as He reveals it—wash one dish, make one phone call, put on your jogging clothes. Then take the next step...and the next.

- *Have faith that what needs to get done will get done.* Since you have dedicated your day to the Lord, trust that He'll show you the one thing or many things that must be done. Do what you can do in the time allotted. Then trust that what wasn't accomplished was either unnecessary or is being taken care of by God.

- *Be open to the Spirit's leading.* You may find your day interrupted by divine appointments. Instead of resisting the interruptions, flow with the "one thing" as God brings it across your path. You'll be amazed at the joy and freedom that come from surrendering your agenda and cooperating with His.

Commit to the LORD whatever you do,
and your plans will succeed.

PROVERBS 16:3

Make a Plan

Which of the practices from "The Practical Power of the 'One Thing'" sidebar could help you most this week?

What specific step will you take to walk out this principle?

Burden Bearer

Give your burdens to the LORD, and he will take care of you. He will not permit the godly to slip and fall.

PSALM 55:22, NLT

Jesus Came to a Burdened World

Religion had become a _____ that Jesus said was impossible to bear (Matthew 23:1–4).

- When it comes to sin, Jesus is our BURDEN _____ .
- When it comes to life, He wants to be our BURDEN _____.

The Invitation, Matthew 11:28–30

"Come to me, all you who are weary and burdened, and I will give you rest."

Rest means "inner tranquility while engaged in necessary _____."⁵

Two primary Greek words translated as "burden":

- *baros*—"a burden or difficulty"
- *phortion*—"a _____"

"Take my yoke upon you and learn from me, for I am gentle and humble in heart."

A yoke is a symbol of _____.

"For my yoke is _____ and my burden is light."

Our Helper, the Holy Spirit, John 14:16, 26

Parakletos means "Helper"—the One "who is _____ alongside."

Your burden can be a _____ (OT: *yehab*) (Psalm 55:22).

Closing Time

I sense the Lord saying…

Prayer Requests

This Week's Assignment

- Follow through with your week 4 "Make a Plan" homework.
- Read chapters 5 and 7 in *Having a Mary Heart in a Martha World*. (NOTE: I've assigned these two chapters because they touch on related topics; we will cover chapter 6 next week. Groups using the eleven- or twelve-week format should read only chapter 5.)
- Answer week 5 study questions.
- Continue to review previous verses. Memorize **Matthew 6:33**: "But seek first his kingdom and his righteousness, and all these things will be given to you as well."

Living Room Intimacy

She had a sister called Mary, who sat at the Lord's feet listening to what he said.

LUKE 10:39

READ: Chapters 5 and 7 in *Having a Mary Heart in a Martha World*
(NOTE: Because they cover related topics, I've assigned chapters 5 and 7 to be read together. For groups using the eleven- or twelve-week format, read only chapter 5.)

*G*od wants to know me?"

I know it's a hard concept to understand let alone accept, but Jesus came for one reason alone: to reconcile us to the heart of our loving Father. The Creator who shaped you in your mother's womb, the God who has numbered every hair on your head and who knew your days before even one of them came to be (see Psalm 139:13–16; Luke 12:7) made you for one purpose: to know Him and be known by Him.

Everything else is secondary. Your gifts, your talents, your fears, your failings—even your God-ordained destiny fades in the light of this one amazing truth. God wants to have a relationship with you. A friendship that goes beyond Sunday morning church services, ladies' Bible study, and an occasional walk in the woods.

He wants to make His home in you. And He wants you to make your home in Him. God isn't looking for servants. He's looking for daughters to call His own.

What an amazing privilege. What a profound delight.

Memory Verse

But seek first his kingdom and his righteousness, and all these things will be given to you as well.

MATTHEW 6:33

WORD TIME: Bible Reading Highlights

When I first began writing down what I felt God was speaking to me through His Word, the Bible came alive for me. No longer did I walk away, forgetting what I saw (James 1:23–24); instead, the Word began to change me as I found ways to apply it to my life. I invite you to try the approach I've found most helpful in my Bible reading:[6]

1. Read slowly through a chapter until something sticks out to you, then meditate on that portion.
2. As you read, mark key words or phrases with one of the markings suggested in week 4.
3. Use the following template to note the portion you've read and the reference of the verse you've chosen to meditate on. After writing out the verse, journal how it impressed you. You can do this in several ways:
   • Respond to God in prayer and personal application.
   • Paraphrase verses in your own words.
   • Note other verses that correspond with what you've read.
   • If you are confused by the meaning, ask God questions.

Best thing I marked today: _____

Reference: _____

Verse: _____

How it impressed me: _____

_____

You'll find several pages of these templates in the back of this study guide, or use this format in a journal or notebook.

My son, do not forget my teaching, but keep my commands in your heart.

PROVERBS 3:1

This Week's Study

1. It's been said that each of us was created "with a God-shaped hole" and that we will never be satisfied until we fill that space with Him. Read the Spiritual Snickers Bars story on page 69 in the main book (hardcover, page 79). What do you tend to turn to instead of God when you're feeling empty?

2. When we look to something or someone other than God to fill a need in our hearts, the Bible calls it "idolatry." Isaiah 46 gives us a vivid image of what our lives look like when we are weighed down by idols.

   > Bel and Nebo, the gods of Babylon, bow as they are lowered to the ground. They are being hauled away on ox carts. The poor beasts stagger under the weight. Both the idols and their owners are bowed down. The gods cannot protect the people, and the people cannot protect the gods. They go off into captivity together. (verses 1–2, NLT)

   Now read verses 3–4, and note the stark contrast between what false gods require and what our God offers. What differences stand out to you? (If you're feeling artistic, draw a picture of what each Scripture portion depicts.)

3. What is weighing you down? Could it be an area of idolatry—a place where you are looking to something or someone other than God for comfort, fulfillment, or happiness? Write a prayer confessing your idolatry, and recommit yourself to simply being carried in His arms.

4. Beyond the human tendency to look in wrong places for fulfillment, we all face other barriers to intimacy with God. Put a check by the one or two you struggle with most, then look up the verses related to that barrier. Circle the verse that is most meaningful to you.

_____ Unworthiness (Ephesians 2:13–14; 1 John 3:1)

_____ Busyness / Fatigue (Psalm 90:12; Isaiah 40:29–31)

_____ Guilt / Shame (Psalm 32:5; 1 John 1:9)

_____ Pride (James 4:6–7; 1 Peter 5:6)

_____ Depression / Sadness (Psalm 42:11; John 14:1)

_____ Trials / Hardships (Hebrews 13:6; James 1:12)

5. Jesus told Martha, "Mary has chosen what is better" (Luke 10:42), that is, fellowship with Him. Consider the following verses and what Jesus does for us when we choose Him above everything else.

Luke 18:29–30

John 1:12

John 15:7

1 Corinthians 1:30

6. Read the "hoopy birthday" story on pages 99–100 in the main book (hardcover, pages 112–13). List the various hula hoops you're trying to keep in motion. Put stars by the ones that tend to consume most of your time and attention.

7. Making Jesus the center of our lives doesn't just happen; we must purposefully place Him there.

Prayer + **the Word** + *Time* = *Intimacy with God*

Which part of the formula for intimacy with God have you found most helpful in your life? What area would you like to grow in?

8. God longs to have fellowship with us. Read the following verses, then draw a line to the related metaphor Scripture uses to describe the intimate relationship we can have with God.

John 15:5   Son and father

Romans 8:15–16   Husband and wife

2 Corinthians 11:2   Branch and vine

Which of these metaphors means the most to you? Explain.

9. In *Having a Mary Heart in a Martha World,* read the excerpt on pages 71–73 (pages 81–83 in the hardcover) from Robert Boyd Munger's article "My Heart Christ's Home." How does it make you feel to think that Jesus longs to have time alone with you, to be at home in you? How could this realization turn your devotional life from a duty to a delight?

Creative Quiet Times

If you've found yourself yawning during devotions—or just eager for a change—you may want to consider the following suggestions for creative intimacy with God.

1. *Take God out for coffee.* Find a quiet corner in a café and meet with God. With your Bible and a notebook, you're set for a heart-to-heart with your very Best Friend.

2. *Add a spiritual classic to your devotional diet.* While nothing should replace the Word of God, Christian books provide delicious and enriching side dishes!

3. *Put feet to your faith.* Take a walk with God! Praise Him for His handiwork. Listen to the Bible on your iPod. Pray. Your body and spirit will appreciate the workout.

4. *Journal your journey.* Keep a spiritual diary. Record thoughts as you meditate on Scripture. List prayer requests and answers.

5. *Come before Him with singing.* Add music to your devotions. Use a praise CD or sing a cappella. Read a hymn out loud. Praise ushers us into the presence of God.

6. *Let faith come by hearing.* Download sermons from favorite speakers. Anointed preaching builds both knowledge and faith.

7. *Dig a little deeper.* A good Bible study will take you beyond just reading the Word. It will help you rightly divide the Word of Truth and apply it to your life.

8. *All the King's versions.* Find a Bible translation you understand for your regular devotions. Read from other versions to add fresh perspectives.

9. *Hide the Word.* Memorizing Scripture plants the Word of God deep in your heart. Write verses on index cards and carry them with you to practice.

10. *Spend a half day in prayer.* It may seem impossible, but as you set aside a large portion of time to spend with the Lord, He will meet you in extraordinary ways.

Make a Plan

Intimacy with God doesn't just happen; we have to purposely make room for it in our lives. Use the worksheet below to formulate a Quiet Time plan for how you will meet daily with God this week.

TIME:

PLACE:

ANTICIPATED OBSTACLES:

SOLUTIONS:

CREATIVE QUIET TIME IDEAS: As you look at the ideas on the previous page, which appeals most to you? Any ideas of your own?

Pursued by Love

> *I will give them a heart to know me, that I am the LORD. They will be*
> *my people, and I will be their God.*

JEREMIAH 24:7

Jesus, Our Way Maker

We were made for a Garden, but sin destroyed all that. Yet God's love kept reaching...

- God's holiness required separation—the temple _____.

- But then Jesus came as the final sacrifice to _____ us to God.

- The veil was "torn in two from top to bottom" (Matthew 27:51).

Jesus, Our Example

Jesus came to show us the way back to Garden-of-Eden intimacy with God. He modeled...

1. Solitude (Luke 5:16)

2. The Word (Joshua 1:8)

3. Prayer (Luke 11:1)

4. Dependence on _____ (John 5:19)

Finding Our Way Back Home

Because of Jesus, we are invited to enjoy full and complete fellowship with our Father (John 14:23; 17:23).

Our life is "_____ with Christ in God" (Colossians 3:3).

Closing Time

I sense the Lord saying…

Prayer Requests

This Week's Assignment

- Follow through with your week 5 "Make a Plan" homework.
- Read chapter 6 in *Having a Mary Heart in a Martha World*. (NOTE: Groups following the eleven- or twelve-week format should read chapter 7 and use "Bible Reading Highlights" templates in the back of the book as assigned by the teacher.)
- Answer week 6 study questions.
- Plan to start early on your "random acts of kindness" for the week 6 "Make a Plan" homework found on page 58.
- Continue to review previous verses. Memorize **Colossians 3:23**: "Whatever you do, work at it with all your heart, as working for the Lord, not for men."

Kitchen Service

Whatever your hand finds to do, do it with all your might.

ECCLESIASTES 9:10

READ: Chapter 6 in *Having a Mary Heart in a Martha World*

*F*aith without works is dead," James the brother of our Lord tells us (James 2:20, NKJV).

If we say we love Jesus, then our declaration should affect the way we live—not only our moral choices but also the practical ways we love and serve those around us. When Jesus rebuked Martha for her distracted busyness, He was not discounting her need to serve—nor ours. For it was one of the reasons He came—not "to be served, but to serve" (Matthew 20:28).

In order to be like Jesus, we too must be willing to lay down our lives for the needs of others. Whether we offer a cold cup of water in His name or give away something that costs us more than we planned to give, we each are called to be the "servant of all" (Mark 9:35). To be willing to go last rather than first. To minister in the shadows rather than in the spotlight. To live a life marked by an open hand rather than a clenched fist. We are called to give our lives away with holy abandon.

For everything that we have was first given to us by God. We've been blessed to be a blessing, to be God's hands here on earth. Washing dirty feet. Clothing the naked. Feeding the hungry.

Bringing Jesus to our world.

Memory Verse

Whatever you do, work at it with all your heart, as working for the Lord, not for men.

COLOSSIANS 3:23

WORD TIME: Bible Study Resources

We are blessed to live in a time with so many resources available to help us study and unlock the riches of Scripture. Here are a few Bible study tools that have been invaluable to me.

- *Commentaries*—explore the Bible one book at a time, offering insights from Bible scholars who have thoroughly researched the meaning and context of Scripture.
- *Exhaustive Concordance*—identifies every instance a word is used in the Bible as well as definitions of the original Hebrew and Greek words.
- *Parallel Bible*—allows you to compare verses in various translations side by side.
- *Topical Index*—helps you search for a certain word or phrase as it is used in the Bible.
- *Bible Dictionary*—provides deeper insight into the culture, customs, and people of biblical times.
- *Bible Software*—brings these resources and more to your computer in an easily accessible and searchable format.

Many study helps are available online with search engines to help you explore multiple Bible translations, concordances, commentaries, Bible dictionaries and encyclopedias, topical indexes, Greek and Hebrew lexicons, charts and maps, Bible reading guides, even devotionals. Many sites also offer mobile apps. Here are a few you might find helpful:

- www.BibleGateway.com
- www.BibleStudyTools.com
- www.BlueLetterBible.org
- https://Net.Bible.org

Study to shew thyself approved unto God, a workman that needeth not to be ashamed, rightly dividing the word of truth.

2 TIMOTHY 2:15, KJV

THIS WEEK'S STUDY

1. Dwight L. Moody said, "Of one hundred men, one will read the Bible; the ninety-nine will read the Christian."[7] Who was the first Christian in your life to live in such a way that you could clearly see Christ?

   How did this person affect your life?

2. Read the story of the little boy and the evangelist on page 97 of *Having a Mary Heart in a Martha World* (hardcover, page 108). How would you like Jesus to "stick out all over" in your life? Label the stick figure below with attitudes and characteristics of the Savior that you would like God to help you develop in your life.

3. Read John 13:1–17. When Jesus washed the disciples' feet, it was a totally unexpected example of what true Christian love looks like. According to page 82 of the main book (hardcover, page 93), why was it so shocking?

In verses 15–17, what did Jesus say was the purpose behind the act, and what reward did He promise to those who embraced this teaching?

4. J. Oswald Sanders said, "It is noteworthy that only once did Jesus say that he was leaving his disciples an example, and that was when he washed their feet."[8] In what unexpected ways could we "wash the feet" of those around us?

5. Consider carefully the qualities of love found in 1 Corinthians 13:4–7:

a) Patient

b) Kind

c) Does not envy

d) Does not boast

e) Not proud

f) Does not dishonor others

g) Not self-seeking

h) Not easily angered

i) Keeps no record of wrongs

j) Does not delight in evil

k) Rejoices in the truth

l) Always protects

m) Always trusts

n) Always hopess

o) Always perseveres

Make a list of the key relationships in your life. Write the letter(s) corresponding to the quality or qualities you would like to work on in order to be more loving toward each person.

RELATIONSHIP   **QUALITIES NEEDED**

6. According to 1 John 3:14, how can we know "we have passed from death to life"?

Continuing on in 1 John 3, what do the following verses tell us that love should look like?

Verse 16:

Verse 17:

Verse 18:

Which of these is the hardest for you to carry out, and why?

7. Read Matthew 25:31–46, and answer the following questions:

What will Jesus do one day, according to verses 31–33?

What significant differences do you note between the two groups described in the rest of this passage?

SHEEP   **GOATS**

8. From Matthew 25, write out verses 40 and 45. Make note of anything you sense Him speaking specifically to you about these two verses.

9. According to the following scriptures, whom are we to love besides our fellow Christians? Place the letter corresponding to the appropriate verse next to the people we are to love, then describe how and/or why we are to love them.

(a) Luke 6:27–28, 35–36   (b) Acts 20:35
(c) 1 Timothy 5:4b, 8   (d) James 1:27

WHO TO LOVE   **HOW AND WHY?**

_____ Widows and orphans

_____ The weak

_____ Family and relatives

_____ Your enemies

10. Is there someone in your life whom you find difficult to love? In the space below, write out a prayer asking God to bless that individual and to help you love that person better and more.

Make a Plan

This week, let's show love in tangible and unexpected ways. Let's commit some "random acts of kindness." (Planned acts are great as well!) Answer the questions below.

What could you do?

What did you do?

How did it feel, and what did you learn?

Compelled by Love

> *May the Lord make your love increase and overflow for each other and*
> *for everyone else.*

1 THESSALONIANS 3:12

The Call to Radical Love, Matthew 22:37–40

- Love _____ with all your heart, soul, and mind.
- Love your neighbor as yourself.

While *love* is a noun, it is best lived out as a _____ (James 2:26).

Jesus' love in feeding the five thousand (Mark 6:30–44; John 6:1–13).

The Challenge of Practical Love

Principle #1: True love always _____ something.

Principle #2: Do what you can with what you _____.

Principle #3: When we give what we have, God makes it more than enough.

Developing a Kitchen Service Heart

1. Be sensitive to the Spirit's leading.
2. Be willing to do what is _____.
3. Cultivate a holy detachment to the _____.
4. Be completely dependent.

"God [will] make all grace abound to you, so that in all things at all times, having all that you need, you will abound in every good work" (2 Corinthians 9:8).

Closing Time

I sense the Lord saying...

Prayer Requests

This Week's Assignment

- If you haven't already done your random act of kindness, look for ways to complete the week 6 "Make a Plan" homework.
- Read chapter 8 in *Having a Mary Heart in a Martha World.*
- Answer week 7 study questions.
- Continue to review previous verses. Memorize **Romans 8:28**: "And we know that in all things God works for the good of those who love him, who have been called according to his purpose."

Lessons from Lazarus

So the sisters sent word to Jesus, "Lord, the one you love is sick."

JOHN 11:3

READ: Chapter 8 in *Having a Mary Heart in a Martha World*

*H*ave you ever struggled with God's timing?

I certainly have. Nothing is as difficult to bear as the discipline of waiting. It's hard not to lose heart when you are caught in the in-between time—that often interminable gap between our prayer request and the moment we receive an answer.

Mary and Martha must have struggled with doubt and fear as they watched their brother worsen day by day without any sign of Jesus' coming. Their hearts must have sunk in disbelief at Lazarus's last breath. They'd been so certain that Jesus would heal him. But now? Now it was too late. All hope was gone.

At least that's how it seemed. But God, as we discover over and over in Scripture, is never late. Though He rarely arrives early—at least in our human estimation—we can be assured of this: He will always be right on time.

Memory Verse

And we know that in all things God works for the good of those who love him, who have been called according to his purpose.

ROMANS 8:28

WORD TIME: Praying God's Word

In John 15:7 Jesus shares an important link between prayer and the Word of God: "If you remain in me and my words remain in you, ask whatever you wish, and it will be given you." Imagine the power when we pray Scripture over the situations we face and the people we love! Here are a few ways to do that:

- Pray prayers from the Bible.

  And this is my prayer: that your love may abound more and more in knowledge and depth of insight, so that you may be able to discern what is best and may be pure and blameless until the day of Christ, filled with the fruit of righteousness that comes through Jesus Christ—to the glory and praise of God. (Philippians 1:9–11)

- Look for—and ask God to give you!—promises to pray.

  Being confident of this, that he who began a good work in you will carry it on to completion until the day of Christ Jesus. (Philippians 1:6)

- Personalize Scripture for specific needs.

  My paraphrase of James 1:5: "Lord, You told me that if I lack wisdom, I should ask You and You will give it to me generously without finding fault."

- Pray Scripture over personal strongholds.

  For God has not given us a spirit of fear, but of power and of love and of a sound mind. (2 Timothy 1:7, NKJV)

- Read inspirational Scripture out loud as prayers.

  O our God,...we have no power to face this vast army that is attacking us. We do not know what to do, but our eyes are upon you. (2 Chronicles 20:12)

- Pray one of the most important prayers: Jesus' prayer in Gethsemane.

  "Not my will, but yours be done." (Luke 22:42)

Praying Scripture not only has the power to change our hearts and minds; it has the power to change things around us. For God's hand is moved when God's people pray.

My word that goes out from my mouth:
It will not return to me empty, but will accomplish what
I desire and achieve the purpose for which I sent it.

ISAIAH 55:11

THIS WEEK'S STUDY

1. What is your favorite kind of story, and why?

Romance	Mystery	Historical
Biography	Adventure	Biblical
Sci-Fi	Fantasy	Other:

2. Read John 11:1–5. Circle key words, and think about this family's situation and Jesus' response. When you face difficulties, which of these verses might comfort you most, and why?

3. Which lesson from Lazarus, highlighted in chapter 8 of the main book, have you found most true in your life? Explain what you learned.

   • God's will does not always proceed in a straight line.
   • God's love sometimes tarries (waits) for our good and His glory.
   • God's ways are not our ways, but His character is still dependable.
   • God's plan is released when we believe and obey.
   • The "end" is never the end; it is only the beginning.

4. Like Mary and Martha, we've all faced difficult situations that we would love God to change. Sometimes He does. But sometimes He doesn't. What can we learn from Paul's honest exchange with God in 2 Corinthians 12:7–10?

5. Choose a phrase from 2 Corinthians 12:7–10 that means the most to you. Are you facing a problem that needs this truth today? Take a few moments and have a conversation with God just as Paul did. Write it out below, if you'd like. Allow the truth of God's Word to give you a new perspective.

6. As strange as it sounds, blessings often come wrapped in difficulties. Nothing is wasted in God's economy. What do the following verses say about that?

James 1:2–4

1 Peter 1:6–7

7. Paul faced a lot of difficulties beyond his mysterious "thorn in my flesh" (2 Corinthians 12:7) that somehow released God's grace in his life. What do the following verses tell us about other problems Paul faced and the benefits that he experienced in each situation?

2 Corinthians 1:8–10
PROBLEM:

BENEFIT:

Philippians 4:12–13
PROBLEM:

BENEFIT:

In both of these passages, who provided Paul's strength?

8. Consider Laura Barter Snow's words on viewing difficulties through the lens of God's sovereignty and goodness:

My child, I have a message for you today; let me whisper it in your ear, that it may gild with glory any storm clouds which may arise, and smooth the rough places upon which you may have to tread. It is short, only five words, but let them sink into your inmost soul; use them as a pillow upon which to rest your weary head.... This thing is from ME.[9]

How would your life be different if you could rest in the fact that you have a heavenly Father who loves you and who specializes in turning all things for your good (Romans 8:28)?

9. Trusting God is crucial during dark times. But as Martha Tennison says, "We only trust people we know."[10] The best way to know God better is through His Word. What do the following verses reveal about our heavenly Father?

Psalm 18:2   "The LORD is _____."

Psalm 27:1   "The LORD is _____."

Psalm 34:18 "The LORD is _____."

Psalm 100:5 "The LORD is _____."

Psalm 145:8 "The LORD is _____."

Which of these verses did you need to hear today, and why?

10. Look up the word *trust* in a Bible concordance. Find two phrases that speak to you, and write out the corresponding verses.

Verse #1

Verse #2

Make a Plan

In the midst of great difficulty, David writes in Psalm 31:14–15, "But I trust in you, O LORD; I say, 'You are my God.' My times are in your hands."

Is there an area of frustration you need to commit to the Lord today? Briefly describe your situation, then use David's template for prayer.

My situation:

My prayer:

This week, whenever doubt begins to rise or frustration begins to grow, say aloud:

"I trust You, God."

Rewriting History

"For I know the plans I have for you," declares the LORD, "plans to prosper you and not to harm you, plans to give you hope and a future."

JEREMIAH 29:11

The Story Behind the Story

Because we know Bible story endings, we tend to minimize the difficult "middles."

Stories of Faith, Hebrews 11

"Faith is being…certain of what we do not _____" (verse 1).

- Abraham
- Joseph
- Rahab

How did these people survive their stories?

- "All these people were still living by _____ when they died" (verse 13).
- "They admitted that they were aliens and strangers on earth" (verse 13).
- "They were longing for a _____ country—a heavenly one" (verse 16).

What Will You Do with Your Story? John 11:1–44

"Lord, the one you love is sick" (verse 3).

"Yet when [Jesus] heard…he stayed where he was two more days" (verse 6).

1. Run to meet Jesus (verse 20).

2. Surrender the quill of your _____ (verses 21–22).

3. _____ that He is the resurrection and the life (verses 25–26, 40).

4. Let God rewrite your story (Isaiah 46:10).

Notes

Closing Time

I sense the Lord saying…

Prayer Requests

This Week's Assignment

- Follow through with your week 7 "Make a Plan" homework.
- Read chapter 9 in *Having a Mary Heart in a Martha World*.
- Answer week 8 study questions.
- Look ahead to page 81 for the week 8 "Make a Plan" homework, and set aside time to fulfill the assignment.
- Continue to review previous verses. Memorize **John 8:31–32**: "If you hold to my teaching, you are really my disciples. Then you will know the truth, and the truth will set you free."

Week Eight

Martha's Teachable Heart

When Martha heard that Jesus was coming, she went out to meet him.

JOHN 11:20

READ: Chapter 9 in *Having a Mary Heart in a Martha World*

*A*re you teachable?

Developing this one quality has the potential to change our lives in amazing ways. The willingness to learn, even from our mistakes, opens doors to skills yet unmastered. Talents yet undiscovered. And attitudes capable of transforming not only the way we live but, more important, the way we love.

So why does our flesh so strongly resist the discipline of the Lord? Well, first of all, being corrected is quite a blow to our pride. Just ask Martha! Though we know we're not what we ought to be, self-justification assures us that we're not half as bad as some people. After all, nobody's perfect, we tell ourselves. But of all the obstacles we conjure up, I believe it is fear that holds us back the most. Fear that we're irreparable. That change is impossible. That God Himself cannot help us. But when we fall for such lies, we miss the opportunity for transformation.

And to miss transformation would be to miss the very thing Christ came to bring.

Memory Verse

If you hold to my teaching, you are really my disciples. Then you will know the truth, and the truth will set you free.

JOHN 8:31-32

WORD TIME: Think Biblically, Live Biblically

The whole point of spending time in the Word is not to simply read it but to apply it to our lives so that we begin to think biblically. Because until we *think* biblically, we will be slow to *live* biblically.

When, through His Word, God reveals something in your life that is displeasing to Him, don't ignore it; do something about it (James 1:25).

1. Repent quickly.
2. Ask God to help you change.
3. Begin to make new patterns.

Look for principles you can use in everyday life. Allow the Bible to be your authoritative rule of faith and conduct. Let it tell you

- how to *act*
- how to *speak*
- how to *think*

The Bible is filled with hands-on practical advice and principles to help us learn to live as God wants us to live. But none of these rich truths will do us any good if we don't put them into practice.

In Matthew 7, Jesus describes a "foolish man" as someone who hears His commands but doesn't apply them. In contrast is the person who listens and obeys. Jesus calls that person "a wise man" who builds his house on a rock. No matter how strong the wind or fierce the storm, that person's house will stand firm.

When we allow God's Word to set our standards—precept upon precept, stone upon stone—we are building a spiritual house that will endure. Because when we learn to *think* biblically, we instinctively begin to *live* biblically.

But if you look carefully into the perfect law
that sets you free, and if you do what it says and don't forget
what you heard, then God will bless you for doing it.

JAMES 1:25, NLT

This Week's Study

1. Since we're considering how to be more teachable, which of the following best describes the kind of student you were in school?

   Intellectual   Absent-Though-Present   Teacher's Pet

   Procrastinator   Party Animal   High Achiever

   Other: Combination:

   What did you like most about school? What did you like least? How have you carried those likes and dislikes into adulthood?

2. In your opinion, what sort of attitudes and actions would an individual need to display in order to be a truly teachable person?

3. Fill out the "Are You Teachable?" questionnaire on page 76. What did you discover about yourself?

   Which area(s) do you want to work on?

Are You Teachable?

Consider the following statements to give you an idea of your teachability quotient. Answer (U) for Usually, (S) for Sometimes, and (R) for Rarely.

____ I feel comfortable asking for advice.

____ I easily admit when I'm wrong.

____ I enjoy reading for information rather than escape.

____ I'm able to receive criticism without being hurt.

____ I enjoy listening to other people's thoughts and opinions without feeling the need to express my own.

____ When I read something in the Bible, I automatically think of ways to apply it.

____ I enjoy church and Bible classes and usually take notes.

____ I'm able to disagree with someone without feeling like I have to debate the issue.

____ I'm willing to look at all sides of a situation before I form an opinion.

____ I'd rather be righteous than always have to be "right."

Give yourself 3 points for each U answer, 2 points for each S, and 0 points for every R. Then add the numbers. If you scored 24–30 points, you are well on your way to a teachable heart. If you scored 15–23, keep at it! You are definitely trainable. If you scored 0–14, you may need to make your teachability quotient a matter of prayer, because you'll find a teachable heart is one of life's greatest treasures.

Take firm hold of instruction, do not let go;
keep her, for she is your life.

PROVERBS 4:13, NKJV

4. Read Hebrews 12:5–11. Identify four reasons why God disciplines us and four results of that discipline.

REASONS	RESULTS
1.	1.
2.	2.
3.	3.
4.	4.

Which one of these reasons and/or results speak most to you, and why?

5. The Bible is filled with if-then propositions: *If* we will…, *then* God will… What do the following verses promise us if we obey? I've filled out the first one for you.

Joshua 1:8   If…   *I meditate on God's Word and do it,*

then…   *I will be prosperous and successful.*

John 8:31–32   If…

then…

James 1:25   If…

then…

6. God is willing to forgive and change us—even at our very worst. Consider David's prayer in Psalm 51:10–12 after his adulterous affair with Bathsheba. Rewrite this cry for transformation in your own words. Read it aloud to God.

7. Many psalms talk about instruction. Read the following scriptures, and write down the phrases that echo your heart's desire to learn from God.

   Psalm 25:4–5

   Psalm 86:11

   Psalm 143:10

8. In His role as Helper, the Holy Spirit uses many resources to shape us as Christians. Identify the resource mentioned in each Bible passage below, and then describe how God uses it to benefit His church.

Ephesians 4:11–13
RESOURCE:

BENEFIT:

2 Timothy 3:16–17
RESOURCE:

BENEFIT:

Hebrews 10:24–25
RESOURCE:

BENEFIT:

9. The book of Proverbs has so much to say about gaining wisdom. Read
   Proverbs 2:1–8. Which phrases do you need to apply in your life today?

Now read verses 9–11. Which of these promised blessings do you need most
this week, and why?

Make a Plan

This assignment may be the hardest of the entire course, but it could also bring deeper freedom than you've ever known. Carve out a chunk of uninterrupted time with the Lord. With your Bible and journal at hand, ask Him the following questions:

Which quality, attitude, or behavior do You consider to be my greatest strength?

Which quality, attitude, or behavior do You consider to be my greatest weakness?

You may come up with other questions as you spend time with the Lord. Record what you sense He is saying to you, and respond to Him in prayer. Now, if you can work up the courage, take your answers to a trusted friend.

Ask God for a teachable heart, and listen to what your friend says. Don't be defensive. Don't get sidetracked by your wounded flesh or battered pride! Let God have access to those weak places. He wants to touch and change you there. Remember, God only reveals so He can heal.

What did you learn?

The Beauty of Repentance

If we confess our sins, he is faithful and just and will forgive us our sins and purify us from all unrighteousness.

1 JOHN 1:9

A Woman Transformed

Martha was willing to receive rebuke from Jesus (Luke 10:38–42; John 11).

She was willing to grow and _____.

What will we do with the rebuke of the Lord when it comes to us?

Will we resist it? resent it? or _____ it?

What Kind of Sorrow Do You Have?

True repentance involves the right kind of sorrow (2 Corinthians 7:10).

WORLDLY SORROW	GODLY SORROW
Regret	Repent and turn from sin
Guilt remains	Guilt is gone
"I'm sorry, _____…"	"I'm sorry, I was _____"
_____ mistakes	_____ from mistakes
Bondage	Freedom

The Beauty of Repentance, Acts 3:19

When the Holy Spirit convicts you of sin,

1. _____ of sin.

2. _____ what you've embraced.

3. _____ forgiveness.

4. _____ with God and others.

Notes

Closing Time

I sense the Lord saying...

Prayer Requests

This Week's Assignment

- Follow through with your week 8 "Make a Plan" homework.
- Read chapter 10 in *Having a Mary Heart in a Martha World*.
- Answer week 9 study questions.
- Look ahead to page 91 for the week 9 "Make a Plan" homework, and look for ways to fulfill the assignment.
- Continue to review previous verses. Memorize **Deuteronomy 6:5:** "Love the LORD your God with all your heart and with all your soul and with all your strength."

Mary's Extravagant Love

*Then Mary took about a pint of pure nard, an expensive perfume; she
poured it on Jesus' feet and wiped his feet with her hair. And the house
was filled with the fragrance of the perfume.*

JOHN 12:3

READ: Chapter 10 in *Having a Mary Heart in a Martha World*

Leave her alone.… She has done a beautiful thing to me."
Those are the words Jesus used to silence the critics who scoffed at Mary's
extravagant love (Mark 14:6). Oh how I hope that one day the Lord will be able to
say those words about me! I want to lavish worship and adoration on my Savior as
Mary did. Though other people might not understand my passion for God or appreciate my zeal, may that never hinder the way I love Him.

What gift could you give Jesus today to confirm your complete love and com-
mitment to Him? Do you find yourself holding anything back? I'm asking those
questions of myself as well. For I want to serve God with wholehearted devotion.
Spending time at His feet in sweet communion, and then getting up from worship
and anointing Him with my all. Pouring out my life in the same manner Mary
poured out her perfume. Loving Jesus the way He loves me.

Laying down my life in total abandon.

Memory Verse

Love the LORD your God with all your heart and
with all your soul and with all your strength.

DEUTERONOMY 6:5

WORD TIME: Worship and the Word

Do you ever wish you had more words to express your love to God? Here's a secret I've discovered...

God's Word is filled with clues that tell us not only *who* God is but *how* we can worship Him better and more. Scripture can actually become a script of praise, providing the words we need to magnify the Lord in the way He deserves.

For as Psalm 22:3 reminds us, God inhabits the praises of His people. He is literally "enthroned on the praises of Israel" (NLT).

Here are a few suggestions to get you started:

- Make a list of God's attributes—to remind you that He is worthy.
- Proclaim the Word as worship—to tell God who He is and what He means to you.
- Use the motions that accompany scriptural worship—clapping, shouting, lifting hands, bowing down, etc.
- Listen to and/or sing Scripture-based songs—to give voice to the Word of God.

Whatever you do, work on expanding your spiritual repertoire of worship! Don't be afraid to demonstrate your love and gratitude to God by using all that you are. Because God is worthy, my friend, and He longs for your love. Just as He longs for mine.

I will praise you, O LORD, with all my heart;
I will tell of all your wonders.

PSALM 9:1

THIS WEEK'S STUDY

1. Read John 12:1–3. Have you ever felt so extraordinarily grateful or passionate about something that, like Mary, you just had to express yourself in an outward way? Describe that moment.

2. Read 2 Samuel 6:12–15, which tells the story of King David bringing the ark of the covenant back to Jerusalem after many years of exile. What extravagant acts of worship do you see in these verses?

3. In 2 Samuel 6:16–20 we read about the response of David's wife Michal. Why do you think she reacted the way she did?

4. So often, we don't express our love and worship extravagantly because we are worried about what other people might think. What can we learn from David's example of worship and his response to Michal's criticism in verses 21–22?

5. Read John 12:4–6. What was Judas's response to Mary's extravagant love?

What did John identify in verse 6 as the motivation behind Judas's response?

6. On pages 164–66 in *Having a Mary Heart* (hardcover, pages 182–84), I highlight the differences between the hearts of Mary and Judas. Consider the lists below:

MARY...	JUDAS...
had a heart of gratitude	had a heart of greed
came with abandon	came with agenda
heard what Jesus said and responded	heard but did not understand
held nothing back	gave nothing up

What impresses you most about Mary's love?

Which aspect of Judas's response sometimes taints your own love?

7. Two gospel writers (Matthew and Mark) place Judas's dark change of heart as happening immediately after Mary's extravagant act of love. According to each of the following verses, why are greed and the love of money so dangerous?

Matthew 6:24

1 Timothy 6:9–10

James 4:1–4

8. In Acts 20:35, Paul quotes Jesus' words: "It is more blessed to give than to receive." Why do you think it's so important to live with an open hand rather than a clenched fist?

9. In Mark 14:3–9, we find another account of Mary's anointing of Jesus. Finish the following statements Jesus made about her extravagant love in verses 6–9:

"She has done a _____ thing to me."

"She did what she _____."

"She poured perfume…to prepare for my _____."

"Wherever the gospel is preached…, what she has _____ will also be told."

Meditate on one of these statements. Ask the Lord to show you practical ways you could love Him more sacrificially, and make note of all He brings to mind.

10. I believe Mary loved extravagantly because she had experienced firsthand the extravagant love of God. Read 1 John 3:1 and Romans 8:31–32. Write a love letter to God expressing your gratitude for His lavish love and extravagant grace.

🍂 Make a Plan

In 2 Samuel 24:24, David says, "I will not sacrifice to the LORD...that [which] cost me nothing." True sacrifice will look different for all of us, but here are a few suggestions as you consider how to pour yourself out before God this week:

FASTING. Saying no to our flesh for a period of time—whether by denying ourselves food, pleasure, or an engrained habit—not only pleases God but also sets us free from the tyranny of our flesh.

CROSS YOUR WILL. To purposefully do something that needs to be done, even though we don't necessarily want to do it, develops character and trains us to be obedient to the Lord. No matter what He asks.

GIVE. Look for ways to be generous beyond your comfort zone. For instance, the Lord may ask you to give away something you love or meet a financial need that isn't convenient. Give until it hurts.

SERVE. Often the best way to love God is to serve people. Keep your eyes open for opportunities to lend a hand, to minister unseen, and "[do] for one of the least of these" as unto God (Matthew 25:40).

DENY YOURSELF. Extravagant love always has a quality of selflessness. Turning the other cheek, forgiving when it's hard, going unnoticed and unthanked—all these are opportunities to die to self so that Jesus might live through you.

This week, look for ways you can implement one of these sacrificial acts (or another that God lays on your heart). Purposefully make it a love gift to the Lord.

What did you do? How did it feel?

Loving God Extravagantly

*I tell you the truth, wherever the gospel is preached throughout the world,
what she has done will also be told.*

MARK 14:9

At Home in Bethany, John 12:1–3
Over and over in the New Testament, we read that Jesus returned to Bethany.

• Lazarus _____.

• Martha _____.

• Mary _____.

Scriptural overview of two anointings:
1. End of Jesus' ministry, by Mary in John 12; unnamed in Matthew 26:6–13 and Mark 14:3–9

2. Beginning of Jesus' ministry, by a sinful woman in Luke 7:36–50

Giving a Gift Worthy of the Savior, John 12:3–8
Mary the worshiper became Mary the servant as she gave what she had.

1. The _____ was an extravagant sacrifice.

2. The _____ took extravagant boldness.

3. The _____ was extravagant abandonment.

The Beautiful Result

"The house was filled with the fragrance of the perfume" (verse 3).

"Leave her alone.... It was intended that she should _____ this perfume" (verse 7).

Our Response

Philippians 2:17—"poured"—*spendo*

Don't _____ to your life; pour it out.

Notes

Closing Time

I sense the Lord saying…

Prayer Requests

This Week's Assignment

- Follow through with your week 9 "Make a Plan" homework.
- Read chapters 11 and 12 in *Having a Mary Heart in a Martha World*.
- Answer week 10 study questions.
- Continue to review previous verses. Memorize **Philippians 1:6:**
  "Being confident of this, that he who began a good work in you will
  carry it on to completion until the day of Christ Jesus."

Balancing Work and Worship

Here a dinner was given in Jesus' honor. Martha served.

JOHN 12:2

READ: Chapters 11 and 12 in *Having a Mary Heart in a Martha World*

*T*here is a time to work, and there is a time to worship.

In a sense, that sentence sums up the message of this book. And yet it is only the beginning. For I believe God delights in a life that isn't compartmentalized—one part sacred, the other part secular—but a life that merges the two into one. Loving the Lord our God with all our heart, soul, and mind (Matthew 22:37) and our neighbor as ourself (verse 39). So that worship becomes a generous lifestyle rather than a weekly bless-me event. So that our work becomes holy because, no matter what we do, we work "as working for the Lord, not for men" (Colossians 3:23).

I can't believe we're at the end of this study! I hope you've caught a glimpse of the Father's love for you as we've studied the lives of Mary and Martha. I pray that you've found the Living Room Intimacy you were made for. But I also pray that you've allowed God to point out places in your heart that need adjusting. For He longs to make us like His Son—and that happens best when we obey His commands.

Though I struggle at times to obey, I've found that if I'll daily submit my life to God's rule and reign, Jesus helps me do the things I ought to do. As I cooperate with His grace, He brings the change. And He'll do the same for you, my friend. For He is the Lord of the Process.

Memory Verse

Being confident of this, that he who began a good work in you will carry it on to completion until the day of Christ Jesus.

PHILIPPIANS 1:6

WORD TIME: Half Day of Prayer

Something powerful happens when we set apart a block of time to seek God's face intensively. Here are a few guidelines I've adapted from the Navigator's 2:7 Series for a half day of prayer:

1. *Find a place free from distractions.* A friend's vacant house, a church or conference center, or even a motel room will do.
2. *Bring along your Bible, a notebook, and a pen or pencil.* You may also want a devotional, worship music, and a prayer list. Wear comfortable clothes, and bring a sack lunch.
3. *Stay awake and alert.* Get adequate rest the night before. Change positions frequently. Sit awhile, walk around—vary your position or activity.
4. *Bring a list of requests and needs.* If you have a specific need, bring it before the Lord along with other prayer requests.
5. *Make time to really listen to God.* Be ready to capture on paper anything the Lord might want to speak to your heart.
6. *Incorporate variety in the day.* Read Scripture, pray, plan, or organize. You might divide the time into three parts: (a) wait on the Lord, (b) pray for others, and (c) pray for yourself.
7. *Bring other Christian material.* Spend part of your day prayerfully and purposefully working through a book or Bible study.

Other tips include:

- *Pray aloud in a whisper or soft voice.* Sometimes thinking things through aloud with the Lord is helpful.
- *Make a worry list.* When things come to mind during prayer, don't ignore them; instead, write them down. Ask God to show you how to accomplish what needs to be done.[11]

My heart says of you, "Seek his face!"
Your face, LORD, I will seek.

PSALM 27:8

This Week's Study

1. To set the stage for finding a balance between work and worship, read the teetertotter story on pages 174–75 of *Having a Mary Heart in a Martha World* (hardcover, pages 194–95). What was your favorite playground toy growing up, and why?

2. After considering the "Listening to Your Soul" checklist described on pages 182–83 in the main book (hardcover, pages 202–3), what does your teeter-totter look like when it comes to balancing work and worship? Draw a line to show which way it tends to tilt (if it does).

WORK .... **WORSHIP**

PIVOT POINT

3. On one side of the teetertotter, we find the importance of loving people. Read the story of the good Samaritan in Luke 10:25–37. Describe the ways in which the Samaritan fulfilled the following statements:

He took *notice:*

He took *action:*

He took *responsibility:*

Which of these three qualities comes easiest to you?

Which is the hardest for you, and why?

4. On the other side of the work-and-worship teetertotter, we find Christ's teaching on prayer. Read Luke 11:1–4. Based on the template of prayer Jesus gave His disciples, what elements should we include in our prayers?

Now read the parable and teaching Jesus gives in verses 5–13. What do you learn about our part in prayer and God's heart toward us?

5. What are some practical ways you could lean into the weak side of your teetertotter to bring balance to your life?

6. In chapter 12, I write about the importance of process in our Christian walk. Have you ever heard a great Christian testimony and wished you could have that person's faith, or live as he or she lived? What difficulties did the person face? What was the process that gave him or her the product of great faith?

7. Read the following verses. Describe the process God uses and the purpose He intends.

Deuteronomy 8:2
PROCESS:

PURPOSE:

Romans 8:28–29
PROCESS:

PURPOSE:

2 Corinthians 4:17
PROCESS:

PURPOSE:

8. Read Hebrews 10:35–36 and Philippians 1:6, then consider the following definitions:

   con·fi·dence / 'känfədəns

   noun: 1. the feeling or belief that one can rely on someone or something; firm trust

   2. the state of feeling certain about the truth of something[12]

   per·se·vere / pərsə'vi(ə)r

   verb: continue in a course of action even in the face of difficulty or with little or no prospect of success[13]

   com·ple·tion / kəm'plēSHən

   noun: 1. the action or process of finishing something

   2. the state of being finished[14]

   Which of these words means the most to you, and why?

9. Read Jude 1:24–25. Rewrite this passage in your own words. Read it out loud as a prayer and as a declaration of faith and thanksgiving for God's faithfulness.

10. Back in week 2 of this study, I asked you to rank how you felt about your relationship with God. Without looking back at your earlier answer, take a moment to reassess it now using the same scale. How are you feeling about your walk with God? Don't be afraid to be honest.

RELIGION		**RELATIONSHIP**
Going through		**A growing**
motions		**friendship**

    1   2   3   4   5   6   7   8   9   10

11. Now look back on page 9 of this study guide. How has your answer changed during the past few weeks? While none of us have fully arrived when it comes to intimacy with God, I hope you've experienced growth as we've studied together. What key truths have helped you? What areas do you still need God's help to grow in?

Make a Plan

As we come to the end of this study, how could you better invest in what "lies below the waterline" in your life, both spiritually and practically speaking? (Read the story of Michael Plant and his boat, the *Coyote,* on page 191 of the main book and page 211 in the hardcover edition.)

SPIRITUALLY:

PRACTICALLY:

Remember, developing a deeper life is not a job you have to do alone. Invite the Lord into the process, and I promise you, you will never be the same!

At His Feet

To close out this study, let's do what Mary did. Find a quiet place and sit or kneel at the feet of Jesus. Let your heart soak in His love as you thank Him for His presence in your life.

Remember, Jesus wants to give you all the strength, wisdom, and grace you need to face every single day. But it's only found as you spend time at His feet.

Session Ten Video

Lord of the Process

To him who is able to keep you from falling and to present you before his glorious presence without fault and with great joy.

JUDE 1:24

To Be Like Jesus
It takes a process to make a product, in life and in our Christian walk.
- Justification is being made right _____ God.
- Sanctification is being made holy _____ God.

The process is divine, but we must cooperate with _____ (Philippians 2:12–13).

  Obedience + Repentance = _____-likeness

A Slow and Steady Transformation
"But we all, with unveiled face, beholding as in a mirror the glory of the Lord, are being transformed into the _____ image from glory to glory, just as by the Spirit of the Lord" (2 Corinthians 3:18, NKJV).

1. Take off the _____; be honest with yourself and God.

2. Spend time in His Word (Romans 12:2).

3. Keep your eyes on _____ (Hebrews 12:2).

4. Don't resent difficult pressures or the anvil of trials (James 1:2–4).

5. Let God _____ anything that distorts His image in you.

"They looked to Him and were radiant" (Psalm 34:5, NJKV).

Closing Time

I sense the Lord saying…

Prayer Requests

As We End This Study

It has been such a joy to be on this spiritual journey with you! As we come to the end of the study, I want to encourage you to take what you've learned—both the spiritual truths as well as the practical tools—and continue to develop and deepen your friendship with Jesus.

To help facilitate that, you might want to…

- use the "Bible Reading Highlight" format (see page 109) to journal what you hear God saying to you as you spend time in His Word.
- keep reviewing your memory verses, and consider adding more to your repertoire!
- finish any study guide homework you were unable to complete.
- go back through *Having a Mary Heart in a Martha World,* and mark things that impacted you.

But remember above all, it isn't what we do that brings the intimacy we long for. It is what Jesus has already done. So take time to sit at His feet daily. He will give you all you need—a Mary heart in a Martha world!

Bonus Session Video

Developing a Quiet Time

Trust in him at all times, O people; pour out your hearts to him, for God is our refuge.

PSALM 62:8

The Blessing of Solitude

When Jesus told Martha, "Mary has chosen what is better" (Luke 10:42), He was inviting her to an intimate relationship with God.

"Only one thing is needed" (verse 42).

Roundtable Discussion

Journaling Your Way to Intimacy, James 1:22–25

Journaling helps you...

- to get quiet and _____ with God.

- capture and _____ what God is saying.

- track and record your spiritual _____ .

Start _____, but begin...

Closing Time

I sense the Lord saying...

Prayer Requests

This Week's Assignment

- Read chapter 6 in *Having a Mary Heart in a Martha World*.
- Answer week 6 study questions.
- Plan to start early on your "random acts of kindness" for the week 6 "Make a Plan" homework.
- Continue to review previous verses. Memorize **Colossians 3:23**: "Whatever you do, work at it with all your heart, as working for the Lord, not for men."

Memory Verses

*H*ere are the memory verses I've assigned throughout this study. If memorizing all nine feels like too much, choose two or three verses to work on over the course of the study. The verses are available online at www.havingamary heart.com in a downloadable business-card template so you can print them for easy reference.

Week Two
Come to me, all you who are weary and burdened, and I will give you rest.

Matthew 11:28

Week Three
Do not be anxious about anything, but in everything, by prayer and petition, with thanksgiving, present your requests to God. And the peace of God, which transcends all understanding, will guard your hearts and your minds in Christ Jesus.

Philippians 4:6–7

Week Four
If any of you lacks wisdom, he should ask God, who gives generously to all without finding fault, and it will be given to him.

James 1:5

Week Five
But seek first his kingdom and his righteousness, and all these things will be given to you as well.

Matthew 6:33

Week Six
Whatever you do, work at it with all your heart, as working for the Lord, not for men.

Colossians 3:23

Week Seven
And we know that in all things God works for the good of those who love him, who have been called according to his purpose.

Romans 8:28

Week Eight
If you hold to my teaching, you are really my disciples. Then you will know the truth, and the truth will set you free.

John 8:31–32

Week Nine
Love the LORD your God with all your heart and with all your soul and with all your strength.

Deuteronomy 6:5

Week Ten
Being confident of this, that he who began a good work in you will carry it on to completion until the day of Christ Jesus.

Philippians 1:6

Bible Reading Highlights

Where to Begin

If the concept of Bible Reading Highlights (described in the week 5 "Word Time" on page 42) is new to you, you may be wondering where to begin. All Scripture is inspired by God, but I've found some portions (Leviticus or Revelation, for instance) to be more overwhelming than others. When it comes to Bible meditation and personal application, here are some places you might start:

Proverbs—one chapter for each day of the month

Gospel of Mark—a great introduction to the life of Jesus

Galatians—a concise overview of the gospel message

Philippians—inspiration for victory in the midst of difficulty

James—practical advice for Christian living

1 John—an uplifting exploration of God's love

On the following pages you'll find "Bible Reading Highlights" templates to get you started. Please feel free to photocopy these templates, or go to www.havingamary heart.com to download additional pages in this format.

Date: _____ Portion I read today: _____

Best thing I marked today: Reference: _____

Verse: _____

_____

_____

_____

How it impressed me: _____

_____

_____

_____

Date: _____ Portion I read today: _____

Best thing I marked today: Reference: _____

Verse: _____

_____

_____

_____

How it impressed me: _____

_____

_____

_____

Date: _____ Portion I read today: _____

Best thing I marked today: Reference: _____

Verse: _____

_____

_____

_____

How it impressed me: _____

_____

_____

_____

Date: _____ Portion I read today: _____

Best thing I marked today: Reference: _____

Verse: _____

_____

_____

_____

How it impressed me: _____

_____

_____

_____

Date: _____ Portion I read today: _____

Best thing I marked today: Reference: _____

Verse: _____

_____

_____

_____

How it impressed me: _____

_____

_____

_____

Date: _____ Portion I read today: _____

Best thing I marked today: Reference: _____

Verse: _____

_____

_____

_____

How it impressed me: _____

_____

_____

_____

Date: _____ Portion I read today: _____

Best thing I marked today: Reference: _____

Verse: _____

_____

_____

_____

How it impressed me: _____

_____

_____

_____

Date: _____ Portion I read today: _____

Best thing I marked today: Reference: _____

Verse: _____

_____

_____

_____

How it impressed me: _____

_____

_____

_____

Date: _____ Portion I read today: _____

Best thing I marked today: Reference: _____

Verse: _____

_____

_____

_____

How it impressed me: _____

_____

_____

_____

Date: _____ Portion I read today: _____

Best thing I marked today: Reference: _____

Verse: _____

_____

_____

_____

How it impressed me: _____

_____

_____

_____

Notes

1. Adapted from *Growing Strong in God's Family*, The 2:7 Series (Colorado Springs: NavPress, 1987), 13, 19–20.

2. Adapted from Dr. Edward Hallowell, *Worry: Controlling It and Using It Wisely* (New York: Pantheon, 1997), 79–83.

3. From a conversation with Alicia Britt Chole.

4. Adapted from *Growing Strong in God's Family*.

5. Spiros Zodhiates, gen. ed., *The Complete Word Study Dictionary: New Testament*, rev. ed. (Chattanooga, TN: AMG International, 1993), s.v. "anapausis" (Strong's #372).

6. Format adapted from *The Growing Disciple*, The 2:7 Series, Course 1 (Colorado Springs: NavPress, 1987).

7. Quoted in Philip Yancey, *What's So Amazing About Grace?* (Grand Rapids, MI: Zondervan, 1997), 262.

8. J. Oswald Sanders, *Discipleship Journal* 76 (July–August 1993): 39.

9. Quoted in L. B. Cowman, *Streams in the Desert* (Grand Rapids, MI: Zondervan, 1996), 35.

10. Martha Tennison (sermon, Billings, MT, September 25, 1999).

11. Adapted from *The Growing Disciple*, 84–5.

12. Accessed online at http://oxforddictionaries.com/us/definition/american_english/confidence.

13. Accessed online at http://oxforddictionaries.com/us/definition/american_english/persevere.

14. Accessed online at http://oxforddictionaries.com/us/definition/american_english/completion.

Connect with Joanna

I'd love to hear from you at:
www.Facebook.com/becominghis
or by e-mail
joannaweaver@hotmail.com

You can also write me at:
Joanna Weaver
PO Box 607
Hamilton, MT 59840

Other places to connect include:
www.havingamaryheart.com
www.joannaweaverbooks.com

Coming Soon!

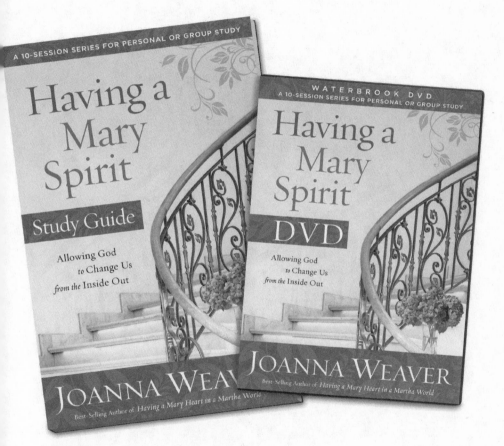

Look for more studies from Joanna Weaver with *Having a Mary Spirit Study Pack* and *Lazarus Awakening Study Pack* coming in 2014.

You were made for more than serving God; you were made to *know* Him

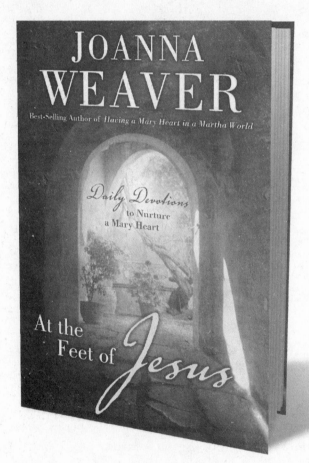

An invitation to connect with God in the midst of your busy day, *At the Feet of Jesus* is a daily devotional that offers you help and encouragement as you move toward a more intimate friendship with Jesus.